L

&

RELATIONSHIPS

QUOTES TO WARM THE
HEART & TOUCH THE SOUL

SUSHEEL LADWA

Author of *10,001 Quotes & Sayings*

ISBN: 1503360091
ISBN-13: 978-1503360099

Mamata and Vishwanath Ladwa

My Mother and Father

"All I Am, I Owe To You"

ACKNOWLEDGMENTS

Writing a book starts as a hobby, becomes a passion, and rules your dreams until it becomes a reality. I gave it time because it is my passion. I want to acknowledge the people that gave their time and support to help realize my passion.

I wanted to thank my wife, Preetha, for her patience, love and support through the blur of day and night with a month old baby. This book would not have been possible without her. Every time there is a knock on my office door, there enters a big beautiful smile that makes it all worth it – Ruhi, my daughter, my friend, my little philosopher and guide. The new bundle of joy of the family – Syon, he is a month old but has shown who the boss is.

My brother, Sunil, my sister-in-law, Sumitra, and kids, Shreya, Kushi, and Arya, for their love and faith in me.

Last but not the least, my editor Jesse Kimmel-Freeman, for all the cattle she chased while editing my book – Thank you!

The laws of gravity cannot be held responsible for people falling in love. - Albert Einstein

A husband is what's left of the lover after the nerve has been extracted. - Socrates

Women are made to be loved, not understood. - Oscar Wilde

Love, cough and smoke cannot be hidden. - Benjamin Franklin

Love is like a virus. It can happen to anybody at any time. - Maya Angelou

Hate cannot drive out hate; only love can do that. - Martin Luther King Jr.

The first duty of love is to listen. - Paul Tillich

Love is friendship, set on fire. - Jeremy Taylor

Better to have loved and lost, than to have never loved at all. - Saint Augustine

A man in love is incomplete until he has married. Then he's finished. - Zsa Zsa Gabor

Love all, trust a few, do wrong to none. - William Shakespeare

Love is the master key which opens the gates of happiness. - Oliver Wendell Holmes

I know of only one duty, and that is to love. - George Bernard Shaw

Dance like nobody's watching; love like you've never been hurt. Sing like nobody's listening; live like it's heaven on earth. - Mark Twain

Man's best possession is a sympathetic wife. - Euripides

Never love something so much that you can't let go of it. - Ginni Rometty

You are what you love. Not what loves you. - Charlie Kaufman

Money can't buy love, but it improves your bargaining position. - Christopher Marlowe

In the end, the love you take is equal to the love you make. - Paul McCartney

Love is life. All, everything that I understand, I understand only because I love. - Leo Tolstoy

Never marry for money. Ye'll borrow it cheaper.

The magic of first love is our ignorance that it can never end. - Benjamin Disraeli

Love means loving the unlovable - or it is no virtue at all. - GK Chesterton

Try as you will, you cannot annihilate that eternal relic of the human heart, love. - Victor Hugo

Real love stories never have endings. - Richard Bach

Love is like quicksilver in the hand. Leave the fingers open and it stays. Clutch it, and it darts away. - Dorothy Parker

If Jack's in love, he's no judge of Jill's beauty. - Benjamin Franklin

Love is needing to be loved. - John Lennon

Don't marry a man to reform him - that's what reform schools are for. - Mae West

Honeymoon: a short period of doting between dating and debating. - Ray Bandy

You have to walk carefully in the beginning of love; the running across fields into your lover's arms can only come later, when you're sure they won't laugh if you trip. - Jonathan Carroll

If thou rememb'rest not the slightest folly into which love hast made thee run, though hast not loved. - William Shakespeare

I met in the street a very poor young man who was in love. His hat was old, his coat worn, his cloak was out at the elbows, the water passed through his shoes -- and the stars through his soul. - Victor Hugo

Where love rules, there is no will to power; and where power predominates, there love is lacking. The one is the shadow of the other. - Carl Jung

Since love grows within you, so beauty grows. For love is the beauty of the soul. - Saint

Augustine

It is impossible to love and to be wise. - Francis Bacon

Don't be reckless with other people's hearts, And don't put up with people that are reckless with yours. - Kurt Vonnegut

As to marriage or celibacy, let a man take which course he will; he will be sure to repent it. - Socrates

Civilized people need love for full sexual
satisfaction.

In a separation it is the one who is not really in
love who says the more tender things. - Marcel
Proust

Sex alleviates tension. Love causes it. - Woody
Allen

If you cannot inspire a woman with love of you, fill her above the brim with love of herself; all that runs over will be yours. - Charles Caleb Colton

The forces that tend for evil are great and terrible, but the forces of truth and love and courage and honesty and generosity and sympathy are also stronger than ever before. - Theodore Roosevelt

Love means having to say you're sorry every fifteen minutes. - John Lennon

Love has reasons which reason cannot understand. - Blaise Pascal

Love is a canvas furnished by nature and embroidered by imagination. - Francois Marie Arouet (Voltaire)

We can do no great things only small things with great love.

No human relation gives one possession in another...every two souls are absolutely

different. In friendship and in love, the two side by side raise hands together to find what one cannot reach alone. - Kahlil Gibran

Hatred does not cease by hatred at any time; hatred ceases by love.

God loves each of us as if there were only one of us. - Saint Augustine

Mortal lovers must not try to remain at the first step; for lasting passion is the dream of a harlot

and from it we wake in despair. - C.S. Lewis

For small creatures such as we the vastness is bearable only through love. - Carl Sagan

Time is too slow for those who wait, too swift for those who fear, too long for those who grieve, too short for those who rejoice, but for those who love, time is eternity. - Henry Van Dyke

Yet each man kills the thing he loves, from all

let this be heard. Some does it with a bitter look, some with a flattering word. The coward does it with a kiss the brave man with the sword. - Oscar Wilde

Love is an ideal thing, marriage a real thing; a confusion of the real with the ideal never goes unpunished. - Johann Wolfgang von Goethe

Don't knock masturbation; it's sex with someone I love. - Woody Allen

Take time to love and be loved, for it is the greatest gift of life.

Love at first sight is easy to understand; it's when two people have been looking at each other for a lifetime that it becomes a miracle. - Amy Bloom

Looking back, I have this to regret, that too often when I loved, I did not say so. - David Grayson

Immature love says: 'I love you because I need you.' Mature love says: 'I need you because I love you. - Erich Fromm

How on earth are you ever going to explain in terms of chemistry and physics so important a biological phenomenon as first love? - Albert Einstein

Love's always a little lonely in the beginning. - Douglas Sirk

Love is energy of life. - Robert Browning

I never knew how to worship until I knew how to love. - Henry Ward Beecher

If you would be loved, love and be lovable. - Benjamin Franklin

Love is that condition in which the happiness of another person is essential to your own. - Robert Heinlein

In his younger days a man dreams of possessing the heart of the woman whom he loves; later, the feeling that he possesses the heart of a woman may be enough to make him fall in love with her. - Marcel Proust

Women love us for our defects. If we have enough of them, they will forgive us everything, even our gigantic intellects. - Oscar Wilde

He that falls in love with himself will have no rivals. - Benjamin Franklin

The love we give away is the only love we keep.
- Elbert Hubbard

In true love the smallest distance is too great,
and the greatest distance can be bridged. - Hans
Nouwens

Love is an irresistible desire to be irresistibly
desired. - Robert Frost

Heav'n hath no rage like love to hatred turn'd,
Nor Hell a fury, like a woman scorn'd. - William
Congreve

Love looks through a telescope; envy, through a
microscope. - Josh Billings

Love lives by giving and forgiving. Self lives by
getting and forgetting. Love is selflessness, Self
is lovelessness.

It's strange that words are so inadequate. Yet,

like the asthmatic struggling for breath, so the lover must struggle for words. - T.S. Eliot

Pure love and suspicion cannot dwell together: at the door where the latter enters, the former makes its exit. - Alexandre Dumas

Love is space and time measured by the heart. - Marcel Proust

Next to love, sympathy is the divinest passion of the human heart.

The greatest pleasure of life is love. - William
Temple

Love is a gross exaggeration of the difference
between one person and everybody else. -
George Bernard Shaw

The giving of love is an education in itself. -
Eleanor Roosevelt

Expansion means life, love is expansion. Love is therefore the only kind of life. He who loves lives. - Swami Vivekananda

Love yourself first and everything else falls into line. You really have to love yourself to get anything done in this world. - Lucille Ball

The supreme happiness of life is the conviction of being loved for yourself or more correctly, being loved inspite of yourself.

Courage is like love; it must have hope for nourishment. - Napoleon Bonaparte

Love sought is good, but given unsought is better. - William Shakespeare

Intense love does not measure, it just gives. - Mother Teresa

First love is only a little foolishness and a lot of curiosity. - George Bernard Shaw

Love is the delightful interval between meeting
a beautiful girl and discovering that she looks
like a haddock. - John Barrymore

Men always want to be a woman's first love;
women have a more subtle instinct: what they
like is to be a man's last romance. - Oscar Wilde

Age does not protect you from love, but love to
some extent protects you from age. - Jeanne
Moreau

People who are not in love fail to understand how an intelligent man can suffer because of a very ordinary woman. This is like being surprised that anyone should be stricken with cholera because of a creature so insignificant as the comma bacillus. - Marcel Proust

It is not the lack of love, but a lack of friendship that makes unhappy marriages. - Friedrich Nietzsche

Love is the answer, but while you are waiting for the answer, sex raises some pretty good

questions. - Woody Allen

Love is composed of a single soul inhabiting two bodies. - Aristotle

Love is agrowing, to full constant light; and his first minute, after noon, is night. - John Donne

Love takes up where knowledge leaves off. - Thomas Aquinas

Real loss is only possible when you love something more than you love yourself. - Robin Williams

Life in abundance comes only through great love. - Elbert Hubbard

Love is like war: easy to begin but very hard to stop. - Henry Mencken

Love is, above all, the gift of oneself. - Bertrand Russell

The greatest happiness of life is the conviction that we are loved, loved for ourselves, or rather, loved in spite of ourselves. - Victor Hugo

There can be no deep disappointment where there is not deep love. - Martin Luther King Jr.

Love seems the swiftest, but it is the slowest of all growths. No man or woman really knows

what perfect love is until they have been married a quarter of a century. - Mark Twain

You can't buy love, but you can pay heavily for it. - Henny Youngman

It is most unwise for people in love to marry. - George Bernard Shaw

There is more hunger in the world for love and appreciation than for bread. - Mother Teresa

Whoso loves believes the impossible. - Elizabeth Barrett Browning

The best portion of a good man's life is little, nameless, unremembered acts of kindness and love.

He who loves 50 people has 50 woes; he who loves no one has no woes. - Siddhartha Buddha

Love is like an hourglass, with the heart filling up as the brain empties. - Jules Renard

Life is one fool thing after another where as love is two fool things after each other. - Oscar Wilde

It is not a lack of love, but a lack of friendship that makes unhappy marriages. - Friedrich Nietzsche

Where there's marriage without love, there will be love without marriage. - Benjamin Franklin

My wife is as handsome as when she was a girl, and I fell in love with her; and what is more, I have never fallen out. - Abraham Lincoln

Love, while always forgiving of imperfections and mistakes, can never cease to will their removal. - C.S. Lewis

Love is a sign from the heavens that you are here for a reason. - J. Ghetto

There is only one religion, the religion of love. There is only one language, the language of heart.

Love is a verb.

A leaf, a flower, a fruit or water poured forth, - offer it with love in thy heart - always accept. - Bhagavad Gita

The fickleness of the women I love is only equaled by the infernal constancy of the women

who love me. - George Bernard Shaw

Absence is to love as wind is to fire; It extinguishes the small and kindles the great. - Roger de Bussy-Rabutin

That is the true season of love, when we believe that we alone can love, that no one could ever have loved so before us, and that no one will love in the same way after us. - Johann Wolfgang von Goethe

If you wish to be loved, show more of your faults than your virtues.

There is no time for cut-and-dried monotony. There is time for work. And time for love. That leaves no other time! - Coco Chanel

To be wise and love exceeds man's might. - William Shakespeare

When I despair, I remember that all through history the way of truth and love has always

won. There have been tyrants and murderers and for a time they seem invincible but in the end, they always fall - think of it, always.

Love is the only force capable of transforming an enemy into friend. - Martin Luther King Jr.

To have the reputation of possessing the most perfect social tact, talk to every woman as if you loved her, and to every man as if he bored you.
- Oscar Wilde

To love means to commit oneself without guarantee, to give oneself completely in the hope that our love will produce love in the loved person. - Erich Fromm

I was in love with loving. - Saint Augustine

A successful marriage requires falling in love many times, always with the same person. - Germaine Greer

It is not beauty that endears; it's love that makes

us see beauty. - Leo Tolstoy

Love is the wisdom of the fool and the folly of
the wise. - Samuel Johnson

Getting divorced just because you don't love a
man is almost as silly as getting married just
because you do. - Zsa Zsa Gabor

Love all, trust a few, do wrong to none

Sex without love is merely healthy exercise. - Robert Heinlein

Love doesn't make the world go round. Love makes the ride worthwhile. - Franklin Jones

Neither a lofty degree of intelligence nor imagination nor both together go to the making of genius. Love, love, love, that is the soul of genius. - Wolfgang Amadeus Mozart

We need not think alike to love alike. - Francis David

When you're comfortable with someone you love, the silence is the best. - Britney Spears

To write a good love letter, you ought to begin without knowing what you mean to say and to finish without knowing what you have written. - Jean-Jacques Rousseau

A coward is incapable of exhibiting love; it is

the prerogative of the brave. - Mahatma Gandhi

Love is not affectionate feeling, but a steady wish for the loved person's ultimate good as far as it can be obtained. - C.S. Lewis

What a profound significance small things assume when the woman we love conceals them from us. - Marcel Proust

Friendship may, and often does, grow into love, but love never subsides into friendship. - Lord

Byron

Love is, above all else, the gift of oneself. - Jean
Anouilh

The essence of romantic love is not the
company of a lover but the pursuit. - Andrew
Sullivan

Love is repaid by love alone! - Mother Teresa

Friendship often ends in love; but love in friendship - never. - Charles Caleb Colton

Love doesn't make the world go round; love is what makes the ride worthwhile. - Elizabeth Browning

Our hours in love have wings; in absence, crutches. - Colley Cibber

We can't command our love, but we can our actions. - Arthur Conan Doyle

Take away love and our earth is a tomb. - Robert Browning

He loves but little who can say and count in words how much he loves. - Dante Alighieri

Love never dies a natural death. It dies because we don't know how to replenish its source. It dies of blindness and errors and betrayals. It

dies of illness and wounds; it dies of weariness, of witherings, of tarnishings. - Anais Nin

Love is the triumph of imagination over intelligence. - Henry Mencken

Young love is a flame; very pretty, often very hot and fierce, but still only light and flickering. The love of the older and disciplined heart is as coals, deep burning, unquenchable. - Henry Ward Beecher

Ever has it been that love knows not its own depth until the hour of separation. - Kahlil Gibran

I have found the paradox that if I love until it hurts, then there is no hurt, but only more love. - Mother Teresa

It's not how much we give but how much love we put into giving. - Mother Teresa

Three grand essentials to happiness in this life

are something to do, something to love, and something to hope for. - Joseph Addison

Absence sharpens love, presence strengthens it. - Benjamin Franklin

Love is the idler's occupation, the warrior's relaxation, and the sovereign's ruination. - Napoleon Bonaparte

Love of fame is the last thing even learned men can bear to be parted from. - Tacitus

Whenever someone asks me to define love, I usually think for a minute, then I spin around and pin the guy's arm behind his back. NOW who's asking the questions? - Jack Handey

They say love is around every corner. I must be walking in circles.

Love is a fruit in season at all times, and within reach of every hand. - Mother Teresa

If you love somebody, let them go, for if they return, they were always yours. And if they don't, they never were. - Kahlil Gibran

Marriage is our last, best chance to grow up. - Joseph Barth

Marriage is a duel to the death which no man of honour should decline. - GK Chesterton

I guess the only way to stop divorce is to stop marriage. - Will Rogers

I think men who have a pierced ear are better prepared for marriage. They've experienced pain and bought jewelry. - Rita Rudner

Marriage resembles a pair of shears, so joined that they cannot be separated; often moving in opposite directions, yet always punishing anyone who comes between them. - Sydney Smith

Let us now set forth one of the fundamental truths about marriage: the wife is in charge. - Bill Cosby

The world has suffered more from the ravages of ill-advised marriages than from virginity. - Ambrose Bierce

Marriage is not a ritual or an end. It is a long, intricate, intimate dance together and nothing matters more than your own sense of balance and your choice of partner. - Amy Bloom

Keep your eyes wide open before marriage, half shut afterwards. - Benjamin Franklin

For two people in a marriage to live together day after day is unquestionably the one miracle the Vatican has overlooked. - Bill Cosby

Marriage is the alliance of two people, one of whom never remembers birthdays and the other who never forgets. - Ogden Nash

A second marriage is the triumph of hope over experience. - Samuel Johnson

Marriage is the triumph of imagination over

intelligence. - Oscar Wilde

It takes two to make a marriage a success and only one to make it a failure. - Herbert Samuel

A successful marriage is an edifice that must be rebuilt every day. - André Maurois

The appropriate age for marriage is around eighteen for girls and thirty-seven for men. - Aristotle

The heart of marriage is memories; and if the two of you happen to have the same ones and can savor your reruns, then your marriage is a gift from the gods. - Bill Cosby

If variety is the spice of life, marriage is the big can of leftover Spam. - Johnny Carson

Marriage is the most natural state of man, and the state in which you will find solid happiness. - Benjamin Franklin

Marriage is the only adventure open to the cowardly. - Francois Marie Arouet (Voltaire)

Ultimately the bond of all companionship, whether in marriage or in friendship, is conversation. - Oscar Wilde

Marriage is a wonderful institution, but who would want to live in an institution? - Henry Mencken

Anger repressed can poison a relationship as surely as the cruelest words. - Dr. Joyce Brothers

Behind every successful man is a woman, behind her is his wife. - Groucho Marx

A man who is eating or lying with his wife or preparing to go to sleep in humility, thankfulness and temperance, is, by Christian standards, in an infinitely higher state than one who is listening to Bach or reading Plato in a state of pride. - C.S. Lewis

You can bear your own faults, and why not a fault in your wife? - Benjamin Franklin

My most brilliant achievement was my ability to be able to persuade my wife to marry me. - Winston Churchill

My toughest fight was with my first wife. - Muhammad Ali

A virtuous wife is a man's best treasure.

The wife is not a the husband's bond slave, but his companion and his help-mate and an equal partner in all his joys and sorrows, as free as the husband to choose her own path. - Mahatma Gandhi

My advice to you is to get married. If you find a good wife you'll be happy; if not you'll become a philosopher. - Socrates

When a woman marries again it is because she detested her first husband. When a man marries again it is because he adored his first wife.

Women try their luck; men risk theirs. - Oscar Wilde

We must respect the other fellow's religion, but only in the sense and to the extent that we respect his theory that his wife is beautiful and his children are smart. - Henry Mencken

Many a man owes his success to his first wife and his second wife to his success. - Jim Backus

Basically my wife was immature. I'd be at home

in my bath and she'd come in and sink my
boats. - Woody Allen

I take my wife everywhere, but she keeps
finding her way back. - Henny Youngman

No man should have a secret from his wife; she
invariably finds out. - Oscar Wilde

Whenever you want to marry someone, go have
lunch with his ex-wife. - Francis William
Bourdillon

The whole purpose of a husband and wife is that when hard times knock at the door you should be able to embrace each other. - Nelson Mandela

What do I know about sex? I'm a married man. - Tom Clancy

My mental hands were empty, and I felt I must do something as a counterirritant or antibody to my hysterical alarm at getting married at the age of 43. - Ian Fleming

It's a funny thing that when a man hasn't anything on earth to worry about, he goes off and gets married. - Robert Frost

If you want to sacrifice the admiration of many men for the criticism of one, go ahead, get married. - Katherine Hepburn

I never knew what real happiness was until I got married, and by then it was too late. - Max Kaufman

A man who desires to get married should know either everything or nothing. - Oscar Wilde

I married the first man I ever kissed. When I tell this to my children, they just about throw up. - Barbara Bush

The average Hollywood film star's ambition is to be admired by an American, courted by an Italian, married to an Englishman, and have a French boyfriend. - Katharine Hepburn

I know nothing about sex because I was always married. - Zsa Zsa Gabor

Married men live longer than single men. But married men are a lot more willing to die. - Johnny Carson

I think that everyone should get married at least once, so you can see what a silly, outdated institution it is. - Madonna Ciccone

And what's romance? Usually, a nice little tale
where you have everything As You Like It,
where rain never wets your jacket and gnats
never bite your nose and it's always daisy-time.
- D.H. Lawrence

Nothing in all the world is more dangerous
than sincere ignorance and conscientious
stupidity. - Martin Luther King Jr.

With money you can buy sex, but not love.

You can't force anyone to love you or lend you money.

I have three treasures. Guard and keep them: The first is deep love, The second is frugality, And the third is not to dare to be ahead of the world. Because of deep love, one is courageous. Because of frugality, one is generous. Because of not daring to be ahead of the world, one becomes the leader of the world. - Lao-tzu

Distrust all those who love you extremely upon a very slight acquaintance and without any visible reason. - Lord Philip Dormer Stanhope Chesterfield

Dignity and love do not blend well, nor do they continue long together. - Ovid

Love conquers all things; let us too surrender to Love. - Virgil, Eclogues

Love does much, but money does all.

One word | Frees us of all the weight and pain

of life: | That word is love. - Sophocles

O tyrant love, to what do you not drive the hearts of men. - Virgil

Love will enter cloaked in friendship's name. - Ovid

The pleasure of love is in loving. - Francois de La Rochefoucauld

The so called negative feedback is often love in disguise. Take full advantage!

Life is short, live it. Love is rare, grab it. Anger is bad, dump it. Fear is awful, face it. Memories are sweet, cherish it.

We always return to our first loves.

The visible sign of utter love is undying smile. -
Sri Sri

Never say that marriage has more of joy than
pain. - Euripides

The greatest day of my life was the day I
married Mrs. Ford. - Henry Ford

He that marries for wealth sells his liberty.

Love lives by giving and forgiving. Self lives by getting and forgetting. Love is selflessness, Self is lovelessness.

A Canadian is someone who knows how to make love in a canoe. - Pierre Berton

I believe that unarmed truth and unconditional love will have the final word in reality. This is why right, temporarily defeated, is stronger than evil triumphant. - Martin Luther King Jr.

The mintage of wisdom is to know that rest is rust, and that real life is in love, laughter, and work. - Elbert Hubbard

If we discovered that we only had five minutes left to say all that we wanted to say, every telephone booth would be occupied by people calling other people to stammer that they loved them. - Christopher Morley

The reason I love my dog so much is because when I come home, he's the only one in the world who treats me like I'm The Beatles. - Bill

Maher

There is a miracle that men can love God, yet fail to love humanity. With whom are they in love then? - Sri Aurobindo

Instead of loving people and using things, we love things and use people.

Force and strife work upon the passions and fears, but love and peace reach and reform the heart.

The odds of not meeting in this life are so great that every meeting is like a miracle. It's a wonder that we don't make love to every single person we meet. - Yoko Ono

I love the man that can smile in trouble, that can gather strength from distress, and grow brave by reflection. - Thomas Paine

There is nothing holier in this life of ours than the first consciousness of love.

Sex without love is a meaningless experience,
but as far as meaningless experiences go, it's
pretty damn good. - Woody Allen

Four be the things I'd have been better without:
love, curiosity, freckles and doubt. - Dorothy
Parker

He who sows courtesy reaps friendship, and he
who plants kindness gathers love.

I have often wondered how it is that every man loves himself more than all the rest of men, but yet sets less value on his own opinion of himself than on the opinion of others. - Marcus Aurelius

The beauty of a home is harmony, the security of a huse is loyalty, the joy of the house is love, the plenty of a house is in children, the rule of the house is service. The maker of a house, is God himself, the same who made the stars and built the world. - Frank Crane

I am a little pencil in the hand of a writing God who is sending a love letter to the world. - Mother Teresa

Love is the irresistible desire to be irresistibly desired. - Mark Twain

Those who are faithful know only the trivial side of love: it is the faithless who know love's tragedies. - Oscar Wilde

Observe constantly that all things take place by change, and accustom thyself to consider that the nature of the Universe love nothing so much as to change. The Universe is change. - Marcus Aurelius

I am certainly not an authority on love because
there are no authorities on love, just those
who've had luck with it and those who haven't.
- Bill Cosby

To be trusted is a greater complement than to
be loved. - George MacDonald

There is hardly any activity, any enterprise,
which is started out with such tremendous
hopes and expectations, and yet which fails so
regularly, as love. - Erich Fromm

All things are possible to him who believes, yet more to him who hopes, more still to him who loves. - Brother Lawrence

Clarity of mind means clarity of passion, too; this is why a great and clear mind loves ardently and sees distinctly what it loves. - Blaise Pascal

Where there is no exaggeration there is no love, and where there is no love there is no understanding. - Oscar Wilde

Divine love always has met and always will meet every human need.

Eventual triumph of good over evil, of knowledge over ignorance, and of love over hatred is the eternal law.

When you arise in the morning, think of what a precious privilege it is to be alive - to breathe, to think, to enjoy and to love.

We cannot all do great things, but we can do small things with great love. - Mother Teresa

As soon as beauty is sought not from religion and love, but for pleasure, it degrades the seeker. - Ralph Waldo Emerson

Certain things, if not seen as lovely or detestable, are not being correctly seen at all. - C.S. Lewis

All the ill that is in us comes from fear, and all

the good from love. - Eleanor Farjeon

An interesting thing has happened since San Francisco started granting marriage licenses to same-sex couples: my marriage is just fine! Even though there are thousands of gay and lesbian couples affirming their love for and commitment to each other, my marriage - my affirmation of love and commitment to (my wife) - isn't threatened at all. As a matter of fact, the only people who can really "threaten" my marriage are the two of us. - Wil Wheaton

An amicable divorce is like a ventilated condom; it just doesn't work. - Rita Rudner

Jealousy is a disease, love is a healthy condition. The immature mind often mistakes one for the other, or assumes that the greater the love, the greater the jealousy - in fact, they are almost incompatible; one emotion hardly leaves room for the other. - Robert Heinlein

One can promise actions, but not feelings, for the latter are involuntary. He who promises to love forever or hate forever or be forever faithful to someone is promising something that is not in his power. - Friedrich Nietzsche

Since love and fear can hardly exist together, if we must choose between them, it is far safer to be feared than loved. - Niccolo Machiavelli

There may be love without jealousy, but there is none without fear. - Miguel de Cervantes

True Love in this differs from gold and clay, That to divide is not to take away. Love is like understanding, that grows bright, Gazing on many truths. - Percy Bysshe Shelley

True love is inexhaustible; the more you give, the more you have. - Antoine de Saint-Exupery

A lover without indiscretion is no lover at all. Circumspection and devotion are a contradiction in terms. - Thomas Hardy

A new commandment I give unto you, That ye love one another; as I have loved you, that ye also love one another. By this shall all men know that ye are my disciples, if ye have love one to another. - Yeshua of Galilee (Jesus Christ)

A purpose of human life, no matter who is controlling it, is to love whoever is around to be loved. - Kurt Vonnegut

All I do is done in love; all I suffer, I suffer in the sweetness of love. - John of the Cross

All men live not by the thought they spend on their own welfare, but because love exists in man.

Always, Sir, set a high value on spontaneous

kindness. He whose inclination prompts him to cultivate your friendship of his own accord, will love you more than one whom you have been at pains to attach to you. - Samuel Johnson

As soon as men live entirely in accord with the law of love natural to their hearts and now revealed to them, which excludes all resistance by violence, and therefore hold aloof from all participation in violence - as soon as this happens, not only will hundreds be unable to enslave millions, but not even millions will be able to enslave a single individual. - Leo Tolstoy

At any rate, let us love for a while, for a year or so, you and me. That's a form of divine drunkenness that we can all try. There are only

diamonds in the whole world, diamonds and perhaps the shabby gift of disillusion. - F. Scott Fitzgerald

At the risk of seeming ridiculous, let me say that the true revolutionary is guided by a great feeling of love. It is impossible to think of a genuine revolutionary lacking this quality... We must strive every day so that this love of living humanity will be transformed into actual deeds, into acts that serve as examples, as a moving force. - Che Guevara

Be patient toward all that is unsolved in your heart and try to love the questions themselves, like locked rooms and like books that are now written in a very foreign tongue. Do not now

seek the answers, which cannot be given you because you would not be able to live them. And the point is, to live everything. Live the questions now. Perhaps you will then gradually, without noticing it, live along some distant day into the answer. - Rainer Maria Rilke

Before you do anything, think. If you do something to try and impress someone, to be loved, accepted or even to get someone's attention, stop and think. So many people are busy trying to create an image, they die in the process. - Salma Hayek

Blue Moon, now I'm no longer alone, without a dream in my heart, without a love of my own. -

Lorenz Hart

Charity - in the true spirit of that grand old word. For charity literally translated from the original means love, the love that understands, that does not merely share the wealth of the giver, but in true sympathy and wisdom helps men to help themselves. - Franklin D. Roosevelt

Curse on all laws but those which love has made! - Alexander Pope

Every man's life (and ... every woman's life), awaits the hour of blossoming that makes it immortal ... love is a divinity above all accidents, and guards his own with extraordinary obstinacy. - Eleanor Farjeon

For one human being to love another: that is perhaps the most difficult of all our tasks, the ultimate, the last test and proof, the work for which all other work is but preparation. - Rainer Maria Rilke

Goodness is achieved not in a vacuum, but in the company of other men, attended by love. - Saul Bellow

Hatred which is completely vanquished by love passes into love: and love is thereupon greater than if hatred had not preceded it. - Baruch Spinoza

Hatred, as well as love, renders its votaries credulous. - Jean-Jacques Rousseau

He that made all things for love, by the same love keepeth them, and shall keep them without end. - Julian of Norwich

I have now understood that though it seems to men that they live by care for themselves, in truth it is love alone by which they live. He who has love, is in God, and God is in him, for God is love. - Leo Tolstoy

I learned the lesson that great men cultivate love, and that only little men cherish a spirit of hatred. I learned that assistance given to the weak makes the one who gives it strong; and that oppression of the unfortunate makes one weak. - Booker T. Washington

I like not only to be loved, but also to be told that I am loved. I am not sure that you are of the same mind. But the realm of silence is large enough beyond the grave. This is the world of light and speech, and I shall take leave to tell you that you are very dear. - George Eliot

I observed, 'Love is the fulfilling of the law, the end of the commandment.' It is not only 'the first and great' command, but all the commandments in one. 'Whatsoever things are just, whatsoever things are pure, if there be any virtue, if there be any praise,' they are all comprised in this one word, love. - John Wesley

I want to break out - to leave this cycle of infection and death. I want to be taken in love:

so taken that you and I, and death, and life, will
be gathered inseparable, into the radiance of
what we would become… - Thomas Pynchon

I will have poetry in my life. And adventure.
And love. Love above all. No … not the artful
postures of love, not playful and poetical games
of love for the amusement of an evening, but
love that… overthrows life. Unbiddable,
ungovernable - like a riot in the heart, and
nothing to be done, come ruin or rapture. Love -
like there has never been in a play. - Tom
Stoppard

If any such lover be in earth which is
continually kept from falling, I know it not: for
it was not shewed me. But this was shewed:

that in falling and in rising we are ever preciously kept in one Love. - Julian of Norwich

If there is one thing Voldemort cannot understand, it is love. - J. K. Rowling

If there's not love present, it's much, much harder to function. When there's love present, it's easier to deal with life. - Brian Wilson

I'm sure we all agree that we ought to love one another, and I know there are people in the

world who do not love their fellow human beings - and I hate people like that! - Tom Lehrer

In all living nature (and perhaps also in that which we consider as dead) love is the motive force which drives the creative activity in the most diverse directions. - P. D. Ouspensky

In hatred as in love, we grow like the thing we brood upon. What we loathe, we graft into our very soul. - Mary Renault

Is it an excellence in your love that it can love only the extraordinary, the rare? If it were love's merit to love the extraordinary, then God would be - if I dare say so - perplexed, for to Him the extraordinary does not exist at all. The merit of being able to love only the extraordinary is therefore more like an accusation, not against the extraordinary nor against love, but against the love which can love only the extraordinary. Perfection in the object is not perfection in the love. Erotic love is determined by the object; friendship is determined by the object; only love of one's neighbor is determined by love. Therefore genuine love is recognizable by this, that its object is without any of the more definite qualifications of difference, which means that this love is recognizable only by love. - Søren Kierkegaard

Is there not glory enough in living the days

given to us? You should know there is adventure in simply being among those we love and the things we love, and beauty, too. - Lloyd Alexander

It costs so much to be a full human being that there are very few who have the enlightenment, or the courage, to pay the price One has to abandon altogether the search for security, and reach out to the risk of living with both arms. One has to embrace the world like a lover, and yet demand no easy return of love. One has to accept pain as a condition of existence. One has to court doubt and darkness as the cost of knowing. One needs a will stubborn in conflict, but apt always to the total acceptance of every consequence of living and dying. - Morris West

It is best to love wisely, no doubt; but to love foolishly is better than not to be able to love at all. - William Makepeace Thackeray

It is better to be hated for what you are than loved for what you are not. - André Gide

It is love alone that gives worth to all things. - St. Teresa of Avila (Teresa de Jesœs)

It is necessary that I climb very high because of my love for you, and upon the heights there is

silence. - James Branch Cabell

It is not earthly rank, nor birth, nor nationality, nor religious privilege, which proves that we are members of the family of God; it is love, a love that embraces all humanity. - Ellen G. White

It is sad not to be loved, but it is much sadder not to be able to love. - Miguel de Unamuno

It takes courage to love, but pain through love

is the purifying fire which those who love generously know. We all know people who are so much afraid of pain that they shut themselves up like clams in a shell and, giving out nothing, receive nothing and therefore shrink until life is a mere living death. - Eleanor Roosevelt

Life on earth is a hand-to-hand mortal combat... between the law of love and the law of hate. - José Mart

Life will not perish! It will begin anew with love; it will start out naked and tiny; it will take root in the wilderness, and to it all that we did and built will mean nothing - our towns and factories, our art, our ideas will all mean

nothing, and yet life will not perish! Only we have perished. Our houses and machines will be in ruins, our systems will collapse, and the names of our great will fall away like dry leaves. Only you, love, will blossom on this rubbish heap and commit the seed of life to the winds. - Karel Čapek

Love alone is capable of uniting living beings in such a way as to complete and fulfill them, for it alone takes them and joins them by what is deepest in themselves. - Pierre Teilhard de Chardin

Love and compassion are necessities, not luxuries. Without them humanity cannot survive. - Tenzin Gyatso, 14th Dalai Lama

Love and music and happiness and family, that's what it's all about. I believe in these things. It would be awful not to, wouldn't it? - Julie Andrews

Love does not dominate, it cultivates. And that is more. - Johann Wolfgang von Goethe

Love has always been the most important business in my life, I should say the only one. - Stendhal

Love has no uttermost, as the stars have no number and the sea no rest. - Eleanor Farjeon

Love is an act of endless forgiveness, a tender look which becomes a habit. - Peter Ustinov

Love is like some fresh spring, first a stream and then a river, changing its aspect and its nature as it flows to plunge itself in some boundless ocean, where restricted natures only find monotony, but where great souls are engulfed in endless contemplation. - Honoré de Balzac

Love is the every only god. - E. E. Cummings

Love is the extremely difficult realisation that something other than oneself is real. Love, and so art and morals, is the discovery of reality. - Iris Murdoch

Love is the magician, the enchanter, that changes worthless things to Joy, and makes royal kings and queens of common clay. It is the perfume of that wondrous flower, the heart, and without that sacred passion, that divine swoon, we are less than beasts; but with it, earth

is heaven, and we are gods. - Robert G. Ingersoll

Love is the most important thing in the world. It may be important to great thinkers to examine the world, to explain and despise it. But I think it is only important to love the world, not to despise it, not for us to hate each other, but to be able to regard the world and ourselves and all beings with love, admiration and respect. - Hermann Hesse

Love loves to love love. - James Joyce in Ulysses

Love many things, for therein lies the true strength, and whosoever loves much performs much, and can accomplish much, and what is done in love is done well. - Vincent van Gogh

Love me for love's sake, that evermore thou may'st love on, through love's eternity. - Elizabeth Barrett Browning

Love, I find is like singing. Everybody can do enough to satisfy themselves, though it may not impress the neighbors as being very much. - Zora Neale Hurston

Love, whether newly born, or aroused from a deathlike slumber, must always create sunshine, filling the heart so full of radiance, that it overflows upon the outward world. - Nathaniel Hawthorne

Love, work and knowledge are the well-springs of our life. They should also govern it. - Wilhelm Reich

Once for all, then, a short precept is given thee: Love, and do what thou wilt: whether thou hold thy peace, through love hold thy peace; whether thou cry out, through love cry out; whether thou correct, through love correct;

whether thou spare, through love do thou spare: let the root of love be within, of this root can nothing spring but what is good. - Augustine of Hippo

One makes mistakes; that is life. But it is never a mistake to have loved. - Romain Rolland

One thing only is needful: the knowledge of the simple and clear truth which finds place in every soul that is not stupefied by religious and scientific superstitions - the truth that for our life one law is valid - the law of love, which brings the highest happiness to every individual as well as to all mankind. Free your minds from those overgrown, mountainous imbecilities which hinder your recognition of it, and at once the truth will emerge from amid the pseudo-religious nonsense that has been smothering it: the indubitable, eternal truth inherent in man, which is one and the same in all the great religions of the world. It will in due time emerge and make its way to general recognition, and the nonsense that has obscured it will disappear of itself, and with it will go the evil from which humanity now suffers. - Leo Tolstoy

One's life has value so long as one attributes value to the life of others, by means of love, friendship, indignation and compassion. - Simone de Beauvoir

Only he who has measured the dominion of

force, and knows how not to respect it, is
capable of love and justice. - Simone Weil

Only the liberation of the natural capacity for
love in human beings can master their sadistic
destructiveness. - Wilhelm Reich

Only tragedy allows the release of love and
grief never normally seen. - Kate Bush

Physics isn't the most important thing. Love is. -
Richard Feynman

Seize the moments of happiness, love and be loved! That is the only reality in the world, all else is folly. It is the one thing we are interested in here. - Leo Tolstoy

Spread love everywhere you go; first of all in your house. Give love to your children, to your wife or husband, to a next door neighbor. Let no one ever come to you without leaving better and happier. Be the living expression of God's kindness; kindness in your face, kindness in your eyes, kindness in your smile. - Mother Teresa

That best portion of a good man's life, - His little, nameless, unremembered acts of kindness and of love. - William Wordsworth

The eyes of fear want you to put bigger locks on your doors, buy guns, close yourself off. The eyes of love, instead, see all of us as one. - Bill Hicks

The greatest thing you'll ever learn is just to love and be loved in return. - Eden Ahbez

The heart unites whatever the mind separates, pushes on beyond the arena of necessity and transmutes the struggle into love. - Nikos Kazantzakis

The length of one's days matters less than the love of one's family and friends. - Gerald Ford

The love of liberty is the love of others; the love of power is the love of ourselves. - William Hazlitt

The more you love, the more you can love - and the more intensely you love. Nor is there any limit on how many you can love. If a person had time enough, he could love all of that majority who are decent and just. - Robert A. Heinlein

The opposite of love is not hate, it's indifference. The opposite of art is not ugliness, it's indifference. The opposite of faith is not heresy, it's indifference. And the opposite of life is not death, it's indifference. - Elie Wiesel

The truth is that there is only one terminal dignity - love. And the story of a love is not important - what is important is that one is capable of love. It is perhaps the only glimpse

we are permitted of eternity. - Helen Hayes

There is no sincerer love than the love of food. -
George Bernard Shaw

There is no sudden entrance into Heaven. Slow
is the ascent by the path of Love. - Ella Wheeler
Wilcox

There is nothing better or more necessary than
love. - John of the Cross

There is only one thing infamous in love, and that is a falsehood. - Paul Bourget

To fear love is to fear life, and those who fear life are already three parts dead. - Bertrand Russell

True love ennobles and dignifies the material labors of life; and homely services rendered for love's sake have in them a poetry that is immortal. - Harriet Beecher Stowe

We ourselves shall be loved for a while and forgotten. But the love will have been enough; all those impulses of love return to the love that made them. Even memory is not necessary for love. There is a land of the living and a land of the dead and the bridge is love, the only survival, the only meaning. - Thornton Wilder

We wanted to bring some love to the world. I thought we were good at doing that. Bringin' love to the world. - Brian Wilson

What is all that men have done and thought

over thousands of years, compared with one
moment of love. But in all Nature, too, it is what
is nearest to perfection, what is most divinely
beautiful! There all stairs lead from the
threshold of life. From there we come, to there
we go. - Friedrich Hölderlin

What is done out of love always takes place
beyond good and evil. - Friedrich Nietzsche

What is needed is a realization that power
without love is reckless and abusive, and love
without power is sentimental and anemic.
Power at its best is love implementing the
demands of justice, and justice at its best is
power correcting everything that stands against
love... I know that love is ultimately the only

answer to mankind's problems. And I'm going to talk about it everywhere I go. - Martin Luther King, Jr.

What really matters is that there is so much faith and love and kindliness which we can share with and provoke in others, and that by cleanly, simple, generous living we approach perfection in the highest and most lovely of all arts. ... But you, I think, have always comprehended this. - James Branch Cabell

When I listen to love, I am listening to my true nature. When I express love, I am expressing my true nature. All of us love. All of us do it more and more perfectly. The past has brought us both ashes and diamonds. In the present we

find the flowers of what we've planted and the seeds of what we are becoming. I plant the seeds of love in my heart. I plant the seeds of love in the hearts of others. - Julia Cameron

When once the mind has raised itself to grasp and to delight in excellence, those who love most will be found to love most wisely. - Francis Turner Palgrave

When one has once fully entered the realm of love, the world - no matter how imperfect - becomes rich and beautiful, it consists solely of opportunities for love. - Søren Kierkegaard

When the power of love overcomes the love of power the world will know peace. - Jimi Hendrix

Where there is great love there are always miracles. - Willa Cather

Your task is not to seek for love, but merely to seek and find all the barriers within yourself that you have built against it. - Helen Schucman

Fall in love, stay in love, and it will decide everything. - Pedro Arrupe

I can think of no better way of redeeming this tragic world today than love and laughter. Too many of the young have forgotten how to laugh and too many of the elders have forgotten how to love. - Theodore Hesburgh

I saw the shallowness of my commitment. I saw the incompleteness of my love. Mine was a negotiated abandonment, and that meant it was not a true abandonment at all. - Anne Rice

It is love that believes the resurrection. - Wittgenstein

It is probably impossible to love any human being simply too much. We may love him too much in proportion to our love for God; but it is the smallness of our love for god, not the greatness of our love for the man that constitutes the inordinacy. - C.S. Lewis

It may be true that the law cannot make a man love me, but it can stop him from lynching me, and I think that's pretty important. - Martin Luther King, Jr.

Late have I loved you, beauty so old and so new; late have I loved you. - Augustine

Life is a mystery, love is a delight. Therefore I take it as axiomatic that one should settle for nothing less than the infinite mystery and the infinite delight. - Walker Percy

Love anything and your heart will certainly be wrung and possibly broken. If you want to make sure of keeping it intact, you must give your heart to no one, not even to an animal. Wrap it carefully round with hobbies and little

luxuries, avoid all entanglements, lock it up safe in the casket or coffin of your selfishness. But in that casket - safe, dark, motionless, airless - it will change. It will not be broken, it will become unbreakable, impenetrable, irredeemable. The alternative to tragedy, or at least to the risk of tragedy is damnation. - C.S. Lewis

Reordered love implanted in a transformed heart is the distinctive mark of the Christian. - David

Take into account that great love and great achievement involve great risk. - 14th Dalai Lama

The cause of all sins in every case lies in the person's excessive love of self. - Plato

The deepest craving of human nature is the need to be appreciated. - William James

The deepest things we know are found in the form of defining affections and passions. A person or a society is better known through what is feared, love, grieved over, and hoped for than through its factually stated ideas and thoughts. - Don Saliers

The measure of love is to love without measure.
- St. Francis de Sales

The more I'm around people, the more I love
my dog. - T shirt

The problem is, of course, that we are not
naturally very good at the love which will make
a long marriage beautiful - even when we try. -
Dick Keyes

The worth and excellency of a soul is to be measured by the object of its love. - Henry Scougal

There are only three great puzzles in the world. The puzzle of love, the puzzle of death, and between each of these and part of both of them, the puzzle of God. God is the greatest puzzle of all. - Niall William

There is no better laboratory for learning to love than ministry. There is also no better place to learn the art of forgiveness than in the life of the church. The church is filled with people. People are broken and sinful. Spend enough time in the church and you will be hurt. - Kevin Harney

To keep your marriage brimming, With love in the living cup, Whenever you're wrong admit it, Whenever you're right, shut up. - Ogden Nash

To love at all is to be vulnerable. Love anything, and your heart will certainly be wrung and possibly broken. - C.S. Lewis

We have all known the long loneliness and we have learned that the only solution is love and that love comes with community. - Dorothy Day

Whoever marries the spirit of this age will find himself a widower in the next. - William Inge

I'm a great housekeeper: I get divorced, I keep the house. - Zsa Zsa Gabor

I'm not upset about my divorce. I'm only upset I'm not a widow. - Roseanne Barr

The difference between divorce and legal separation is that a legal separation gives a husband time to hide his money. - Johnny Carson

Ah, yes, divorce ... from the Latin word meaning to rip out a man's genitals through his wallet. - Robin Williams

It is an interesting law of romance that a truly strong woman will choose a strong man who disagrees with her over a weak one who goes along. Strength demands intelligence, intelligence demands stimulation, and weakness is boring. It is better to find a partner you can contend with for a lifetime than one who accommodates you because he doesn't

really care. - Roger Ebert

Wedding: a ceremony at which two persons undertake to become one, one undertakes to become nothing, and nothing undertakes to become supportable. - Ambrose Bierce

What is a wedding? Webster's dictionary defines a wedding as 'the process of removing weeds from one's garden.' - Homer Simpson

In domestic affairs I defer to my wife Katie.

Otherwise I am led by the Holy Ghost. - Martin

What should the wife of saint be called? A martyr? - Frank Earl

I attribute whatever I may have been able to accomplish in life far more to my wife than to anything else and to everything else put together. But I cannot flatter myself that I found her because I was a 'good picker', I believe profoundly that we are guided, led, in such momentous matters. - Henry Ford

When I woke up this morning my girlfriend asked me, 'Did you sleep well?' I said 'No, I made a few mistakes.' - Steven Wright

You only lie to two people in your life: your girlfriend and the police. - Jack Nicholson

God help the man who won't marry until he finds a perfect woman, and God help him still more if he finds her. - Benjamin Tillet

Men marry because they are tired; women

because they are curious. Both are disappointed. - Oscar Wilde

Some marry the first information they receive, and turn what comes later into their concubine. Since deceit is always first to arrive, there is no room left for truth. - Baltasar Gracián

You enter into a certain amount of madness when you marry a person with pets. - Nora Ephron

If you would marry suitably, marry your equal.
- Ovid

Great wealth will marry off even an old woman.

ABOUT THE AUTHOR

Growing up in a small town in India, Susheel heard a story. A child goes to a fair and sees a man selling balloons; he watches the red balloon fly away high into the sky. He asks the balloon vendor, "Will the green balloon fly into the sky as well?" The balloon man says, "Yes." Next the child asks, "How about the black balloon?" The balloon vendor replies, "It is not the color of the balloon, but what is in it that takes the balloon high into the sky."

Susheel has lived with a strong belief that "it is what you have in you that takes you the places you want to go, it does not matter where you come from, all that matters is where you are going."

Susheel has a passion for quotes, sayings, and studying interesting facts about history and their relevance in the modern world. In the past decade, he has consulted with fortune 500 clients advising them on business strategies.

Printed in Great Britain
by Amazon.co.uk, Ltd.,
Marston Gate.